Ainscough's Liverpool

To Harry Ainscough 1922-1997

Published by The Bluecoat Press, Liverpool
Book design by March Design, Liverpool
Printed by Design 2 Print, Llandudno

ISBN 1 872568 64 5

The publisher wishes to acknowledge the
support of Margaret Ainscough and
family in producing this book

Ainscough's Liverpool

Photographs by Harry Ainscough

The Bluecoat Press

Introduction

by Colin Wilkinson

I first came across the work of Harry Ainscough while picture researching in Liverpool Record Office. Individual photographs were classified under street names, though most files only contained one or two photographs, all stamped H Ainscough - Photographer, 352 Herries Road, Sheffield 5, on the back.

A Sheffielder myself, I wondered why anyone would make almost weekly journeys across the Pennines to photograph a city seventy miles from his own doorstep and I made a mental note to call in on Harry on one of my occasional trips to my home town. Somehow, I never managed to fit a visit in and, when I did decide to make contact in 1997, with the idea of publishing his photographs in a book, I was too late. Harry had died earlier that year but his wife, Margaret, was delighted with the idea of a book in tribute to Harry, whom she described as "a quiet man who just loved taking pictures".

Harry Ainscough was born in Ormskirk on 3 November 1922. His father was an agricultural worker and life was grim growing up in the 1920s and '30s. When War came, Harry served in the Parachute Regiment in the 14th Army, seeing service in India and Burma. On being demobbed, he tried various jobs before finally settling at the Sheffield Telegraph and Star, where he worked as a printer in the photographic department. He married Margaret in May 1959 and had a daughter and son. In the early 1960s, he started to take photographs of street scenes in Sheffield, using his bathroom as a darkroom and selling some of his prints to the Central Library. Seemingly encouraged by this early success, he expanded his horizons to photograph other northern cities. His initial approaches to libraries in Manchester and Leeds came to nothing. A terse comment in his log book regarding his visit to Leeds in June 1966 notes: 'short staffed ... short of money'.

Manchester's and Leeds's loss was Liverpool's gain. Neville Carrick, of Liverpool Record Office, selected an initial sixteen prints from the first batch Harry submitted and so began an enterprise that was to continue until 1974. Harry was clear about his objective, writing in his log book: 'no record of materials used, as the venture was started strictly on an amateur basis and no profit was expected, as most of the work was done for pleasure. Continual returns to various streets to rephotograph, in the interest of producing only the highest quality, meant more use of materials than normally apply on a professional basis. As I never expected to cover my expenses, I made no effort to keep, or even request receipts for materials'.

What drove Harry Ainscough to travel to Liverpool almost every week for twenty years? The money he received from the

Record Office did not even cover his expenses but it is clear from talking to Margaret Ainscough that he enjoyed the idea of recording the city, street by street, as objectively as he could. He set out to create a body of work and, in doing so, has left a visual record of the city at a critical time, when old neighbourhoods were being pulled down to make way for a new development plan in which people were being rehoused vertically, in multi-storeyed blocks, destroying the old street patterns and community spirit that had been built up over generations. His photographs graphically illustrate the folly of the post-War plan to create a 'modern' city by clearing away streets and buildings that often only needed careful restoration. Liverpool lost a number of key buildings during this period, such as Central Station (page 6) and the Theatre Royal (page 10), but the greatest loss was of small-scale domestic and commercial buildings. Of no great architectural merit on their own, collectively they gave a scale to the city. The destruction of St John's Market and its surrounding area, removed a chaotic mix of buildings, but this was the heart of Liverpool, with narrow streets and bustling squares, supporting a healthy mix of commercial activities.

Perhaps Harry Ainscough was a few years too late to document the full impact of change in Everton and around Scotland Road. By the time he started his filming, the high rise experiment was well underway. Fortunately, he has managed to capture the dying days of once vital areas such as Great Homer Street and Heyworth Street, before the bulldozer erased familiar buildings and streets forever. There is no doubt that much of the building stock was beyond repair but the multi-storeyed blocks that replaced them were no solution. Ainscough's photographs brilliantly reveal the brutalism of such architecture. The concrete playground of Crosbie Heights (page 50) is an eloquent statement on the blinkered planning that condemned whole areas to wholesale redevelopment, without community involvement or consultation.

Harry Ainscough's record is a remarkable addition to the city's photographic collections. Liverpool is fortunate in having collections illustrating many aspects of its life during the twentieth century but it is essential that such documentation is not left purely to chance. Photographs taken today may appear to have little intrinsic interest but, in twenty year's time, what was once considered ordinary, often assumes a different perspective. Fortunately, Harry Ainscough realised this and the publication of his work in this volume is a belated recognition of his vision and, hopefully, an encouragement to others to follow his example.

Opposite **Ranelagh Street, 27 May 1968.** *The imposing facade has since been demolished and replaced by a nondescript shopping arcade.*

Left **The Magic Clock, Roe Street, 27 May 1968.** *Another casualty, along with the surrounding buildings, in the wave of the city centre redevelopment of the 1960s. The well-loved market area of narrow streets and busy squares, with an interesting mix of shops and small businesses, is what modern planners strive to achieve today. In the 1960s, such a mix was regarded as untidy and old-fashioned. Modern shopping precincts with multi-storey car parks, were considered 'improvements' and essential to the economic future of the city. The recent Queen Square development has created a new city square but lacks the style and variety of its Georgian and Victorian predecessor.*

Great Charlotte Street, 27 May 1968. The last days of the old street market.

Queen Square, 27 May 1968. The heart of the fresh produce market, the area was demolished to make way for a grandiose civic centre development, which did not see the light of day.

Williamson Square, 27 May 1968. The Theatre Royal was one of the oldest theatres in the country, although it had been converted from its original use to a cold storage depot. The building was demolished to make way for a new road fronting Williamson Square.

Mount Pleasant, 16 May 1966. The famous Mardi Gras Club is on the right – soon to be demolished for a multi-storey car park.

St Paul's Square, 29 April 1968. The construction of the JM Centre dwarfs the sad remnants of a once-teeming neighbourhood.

Benn's Garden, 22 April 1968. Some of the earliest merchant housing with its own private entrance, soon to be demolished to make way for the Queen Elizabeth Law Courts.

St Andrew's Street, 16 October 1967.

Back of Trowbridge Street, 18 July 1966.

Springfield Street (off Soho Street), 18 July 1967.

Gaumont Cinema, Camden Street, 18 July 1967.

St James's Road, 16 May 1966. All the housing on the left side was demolished in the 1970s.

Washington Street, 16 May 1966. Another loss to Liverpool's stock of good domestic early nineteenth century architecture.

Nile Street, 16 May 1966. The David Lewis Theatre (now demolished) is on the left.

St Bride Street, 16 May 1966.

Parliament Place, 16 May 1966.

Gibson Street, 4 November 1968. The street made way for unwanted, ugly maisonettes which have since been pulled down.

Upper Hill Street, 4 November 1968. Not exactly Honolulu but Liverpool did boast a Hawaiian restaurant on North Hill Street.

Park Place, 2 September 1968.

Egerton Street, 16 May 1966. The houses have survived but the church on Catharine Street was not so lucky.

Morton Street, 2 September 1968.

Warwick Gardens, 2 September 1968.

Gerard Gardens, 18 July 1967. The new tenements offered a high standard of housing and were popular until a lack of maintenance and changing aspirations finally saw them replaced by low density housing.

Gerard Gardens, 18 July 1966.

Gerard Gardens, 18 July 1966. The central arena was a safe area for children to play in, although the design amplified the noise to many residents' annoyance.

Vauxhall Road, 23 January 1967.

St Martin's Cottages, Silvester Street, 23 January 1967. One of the earliest examples of municipal housing in England, the tenements survived until the mid-1970s.

Medical Mission, Back Burlington Street, 23 January 1967. A grim reminder of the basic level of provision most working-class areas could expect.

Gardener's Row, 23 January 1967. The new Kingsway Tunnel was to deal a devastating blow to the area, removing buildings and isolating it from Scotland Road.

Off Vauxhall Road, 23 January 1967.

*Argyll Place, 23 January 1967.*Once innovatory attempts to improve living conditions, these council flats were showing their age at the time of the photograph.

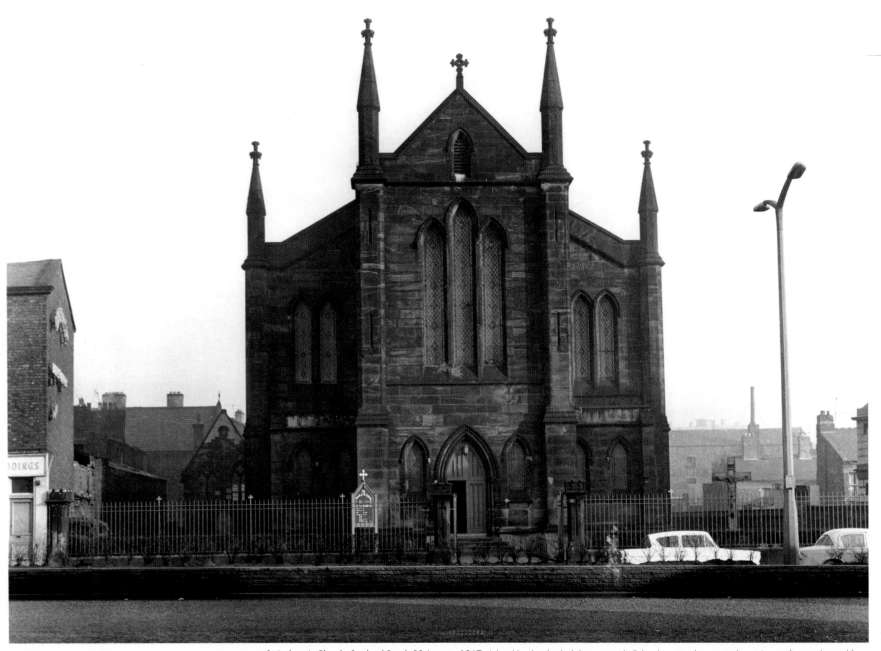

St Anthony's Church, Scotland Road, 23 January 1967. A local landmark which has survived all the dramatic changes to the city's most famous thoroughfare.

Scotland Road, 23 January 1967.

Great Homer Street, 13 July 1967. The area was never prosperous but its once large population could support shops such as Woolworth. Today, most of the people and shops have gone.

Great Homer Street, 3 October 1966.

Jenkinson Street, 22 May 1967.

William Henry Street, 22 May 1967.

Minera Street, 13 July 1967.

Jenkinson Street, off William Henry Street, 29 March 1967.

Off Great Homer Street, 13 July 1967.

Anderson Street, 13 July 1967.

View from St George's Hill, 13 July 1967.

View from St George's Hill, 13 July 1967.

Crosbie Heights, off William Henry Street, 29 March 1967.

Ann Fowler Memorial Home for Women, Netherfield Road South, 29 March 1967. A grim fortress of a building. A last resort for women who had nowhere else to turn.

Browside, 29 March 1967.

View from Browside, 13 July 1967. A panorama of desolation. Landing houses are waiting to be cleared and, to their right, some of the last surviving prefabs struggle on for a few more years.

Heyworth Street, 13 July 1967.

Nun Street, 10 March 1969.

Neaburn Street, 7 October 1965. Before the growth in car ownership, streets such as this offered children a safe environment in which to play

Heyworth County Primary School, 13 July 1967.

Kerford Street, 13 July 1967. Everton was once a prosperous neighbourhood, possessing good quality terraces and villas. Sadly, redevelopment, rather than conservation, was the grand plan in the 1960s and '70s

Everton Road, 29 March 1967.

Upper Baker Street, 7 March 1966.

Vivian Street (off Boaler Street), 7 March 1966.

Street off Boaler Street, 1966. The street is not named in Ainscough's log but such landing houses were once common throughout Liverpool.

West Derby Road, 29 March 1967. Emmanuel Church, with its fine spire, was first to go, followed by the Royal Hippodrome on the right.

Cardwell Street (off Smithdown Lane), 4 March 1968.